KIDDING A[ ]

ATLANTA

A YOUNG PERSON'S GUIDE TO THE CITY

ANNE PEDERSEN

ILLUSTRATED BY JANICE ST. MARIE

Albuquerque Academy
MIDDLE SCHOOL LIBRARY
6400 Wyoming Blvd. N.E.
Albuquerque, NM 87109

John Muir Publications
Santa Fe, New Mexico

for Audrey and Becky Donatelli, without whose help the writing of this book would have been much more difficult.

for Jason from Janice. Thanks for being there.

John Muir Publications, P.O. Box 613, Santa Fe, NM 87504

© 1989 by Anne Pedersen
Illustrations © 1989 by Janice St. Marie
Cover © 1989 by John Muir Publications
All rights reserved. Published 1989
Printed in Singapore

First edition. First printing

Library of Congress Cataloging-in-Publication Data

Pedersen, Anne. 1949-
      Kidding around Atlanta: a young person's guide to the city/
Anne Pedersen; illustrated by Janice St. Marie.—1st ed.
      p.   cm.
      Summary: Describes sights and events of interest in
Atlanta, including the downtown area and attractions
outside the city.
ISBN 0-945465-35-1
1. Atlanta (Ga.)—Description—Guide-books—Juvenile
literature. 2. Children—Travel—Georgia—Atlanta—
Guide-books—Juvenile literature. [1. Atlanta (Ga.)—
Description—Guides.] I. St. Marie, Janice, ill. II. Title.
F294.A83P43   1989
917.58′23104′43—dc20   89-42938
                                                              CIP
                                                              AC

Typeface: Trump Medieval
Typesetter: Copygraphics, Santa Fe, New Mexico
Designer: Joanna V. Hill
Printer: Eurasia Press

Distributed to the book trade by:
W.W. Norton & Company, Inc.
New York, New York

Contents

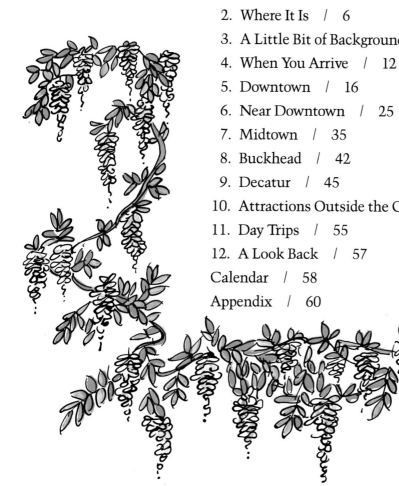

1. Welcome to Atlanta

Atlanta is the capital of Georgia. It is located on gently rolling elevated land (called piedmont plateau) in the north central part of the state, just south of the Chattahoochee River. The city's elevation is about 1,000 feet above sea level. Of major American cities, only Denver is higher.

ou may not realize it, but there are actually several cities here. The one you'll see first is the high-energy, modern one, with gleaming skyscrapers, fancy hotels, and lots of people on the go. This is a city crisscrossed with freeways and dotted with huge shopping centers, a city that hums with activity during the day and is lit up like a Christmas tree at night. The people who live here are proud of this city, and rightly so. It's a boomtown. The greater Atlanta area (called Metro Atlanta by natives) is home to many of the biggest corporations in the United States, and more set up shop every year. Atlanta has more than doubled its size in the last twenty years, and it's still growing at a rapid clip.

But wait. There's another city here, tucked in among the fancy new buildings and busy streets, a city of Southern grace, charm, and history. Peachtree Street, which runs through the heart of Atlanta, was once an Indian trail. One of the most important battles of the Civil War was fought near downtown. The Rev. Martin Luther King, civil rights leader and Nobel Peace Prize winner, was born and preached on Auburn Avenue. Many neighborhoods are full of beautiful old houses and churches that remind you of a quieter, more gracious past. Everywhere, too, are trees and flowers. Once away from the glitz and bustle of the business district, Atlanta feels much more like a friendly Southern town than one of the biggest cities in the Southeast.

Maybe you're visiting because your father or mother is attending a convention here. Or maybe you and your family are just plain tourists. Perhaps you've just moved here from somewhere else. Whatever the case, this book is designed to help you find those places to go and things to do that are of special interest to you—you, not necessarily your parents.

Not everything suggested in this book may appeal to you. People are different: some enjoy puppet shows, others prefer roller coasters. So pick and choose. Great museums, amusement parks, theater, train rides, shopping, restaurants with every kind of food you can think of—Atlanta has it all.

Have a great time!

The population of the city of Atlanta is about 427,000. The metropolitan area (the city plus surrounding suburbs) has a population of approximately 2.1 million. Gwinnett County, just to the northeast of the city, is one of the fastest-growing areas in the country.

Many Fortune 500 companies have headquarters in Atlanta, and more than 1,700 industrial plants here manufacture everything from paper to airplanes.

2. Where It Is

Some major east-west streets are North Avenue, Ponce de Leon, Memorial, West Paces Ferry, La Vista, and North Decatur. Some major north-south streets: Peachtree, Piedmont, Clairmont, Briarcliff, Northside, and Roswell Road.

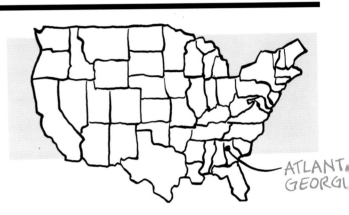

ATLANTA
GEORGIA

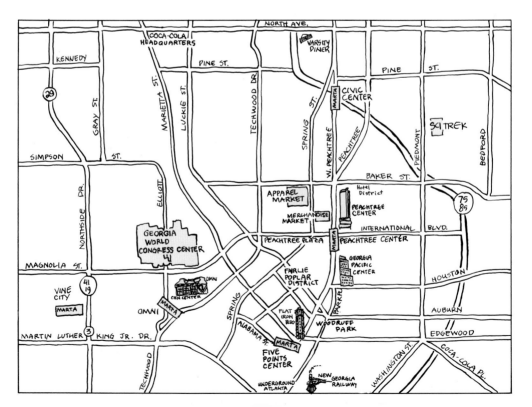

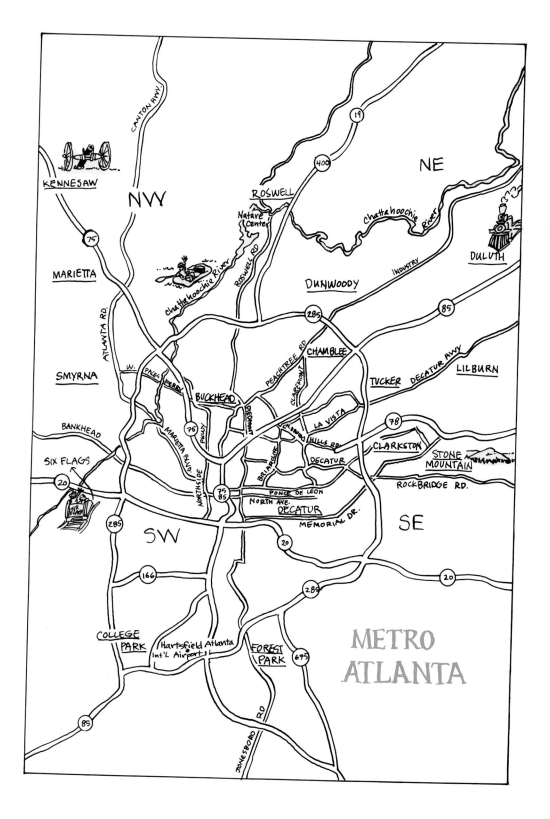

3. A Little Bit of Background

I

Long's original surveyor's stake was driven into the ground near what is now Five Points in downtown Atlanta. The stake itself is long gone, but a "Zero Milepost" now stands nearby in Underground Atlanta.

n the early 1800s, when New York, Philadelphia, and Charleston, S.C., were all well-established towns, what is now Atlanta was just forest and a few Creek and Cherokee Indian settlements. During the War of 1812, the first white settlement, a military outpost called Fort Peachtree, was built on the banks of the Chattahoochee River near a Cherokee village named Standing Peachtree. The Creek Indian Nation gave their lands to the state of Georgia in 1821. The Cherokees held onto theirs, living peacefully alongside up-country settlers until the 1830s.

The city of Atlanta began life as the end of a railway line. In 1836, Georgia legislators, wanting to promote economic growth in the north central part of the state, chartered a new railroad called the Western and Atlantic and gave it authority to lay track from Chattanooga, Tennessee, to a spot near the Chattahoochee River that would be reachable by other railroads. The engineer chosen for the project, Stephen Long, finally chose a place eight miles south of the river, where Indian trails and natural ridges came together, as the end of the line and in 1837 drove a stake into the red Georgia soil to mark the spot.

The new settlement's first name was Terminus,

since it was where the railroad stopped. The Western and Atlantic railroad did not start service there until 1850, but two other railroads, the Monroe and the Macon and Western, soon connected the town to the outside world. The city's name was changed to Marthasville, in honor of the daughter of the governor who had helped obtain the railroad charter. In 1845, the name was changed again, to Atlanta (the feminine form of Atlantic), and the city was incorporated. By 1852, when a fourth railroad, the Atlanta and West Point, reached the city, it was a bustling transportation and manufacturing center of almost 3,000 people, with banks, merchants, and even a medical school. There were also quite a few bars and gambling halls. Atlanta in those days was a rough-and-ready place to live, more like a Western frontier town than the refined, magnolias-and-mint-juleps society we think of as the Old South.

In the 1830s, the state of Georgia took the Cherokee Indians' land away from them. The federal government then used a treaty, which only about 100 Cherokees (out of a total of about 17,000) had signed, to force the tribe to relocate west of the Mississippi River. Thirteen Indian caravans set out for Oklahoma in 1838. Some made it to their new home in three months; others, slowed by disease and suffering, took more than a year to complete the long and painful trip. Out of 16,000 people that set out on this arduous journey, 4,000 died, earning this forced march the name, "The Trail of Tears."

The burning of Atlanta was not entirely the fault of Union troops. Eighty-one railroad cars full of explosives were blown up by retreating Confederate troops so they would not fall into enemy hands. These helped create a spectacular fire, which was reenacted with great effect in the city's favorite movie, Gone With the Wind.

By the outbreak of the Civil War in 1861, Atlanta's population was close to 10,000. It quickly became an important manufacturing and transportation center for the Confederacy. But then, disaster struck. During his infamous March to the Sea in 1864, Union general William T. Sherman evacuated the city and then burned it virtually to the ground. The railroads were destroyed, and only 400 buildings out of almost 4,000 were left standing.

Rebuilding started while the city was still smoldering. Five years later, Atlanta had more than doubled its prewar population. In 1868, it became the capital of Georgia. Growth through the rest of the nineteenth century was rapid. The city staged a series of fairs and expositions in the 1880s and 1890s to bring industry to the area. By 1900, ten railroad lines radiated out from the city, making it the transportation hub of the Southeast. Horse-drawn streetcars were introduced in 1871, and electric ones in 1891. Suburbs popped up: Inman Park, Druid Hills, Ansley Park. A prosperous black middle class took root along Auburn Avenue. Henry Grady, a prominent citizen and editor of the *Atlanta Constitution*, captured the mood of the postwar years perfectly in a famous 1886 speech in which he spoke of a "brave and beautiful city," full of "growing power and prosperity."

The twentieth century has seen more growth. In the 1920s, a "Forward Atlanta" promotional campaign brought more business to the city, and during the 1960s, a building and economic boom began which is still going on. The 1960s also brought the tumultuous social changes of the civil rights movement, changes that affected the whole country as well as the South. During that time Atlanta adopted the slogan, "the city too busy to hate."

Atlanta today is a big, glistening metropolis. Most of it is new, but what is old is cherished. Its symbol, fittingly enough, is the phoenix, the mythical bird that rises from its own ashes to live again.

Atlanta's biggest business success story is that of Coca-Cola. The caffeine-rich syrup that is the basis for the world's best-known soft drink was first concocted by Atlanta pharmacist John Pemberton in 1886. The name was invented by his book-keeper, who wrote out the words in the script that is the company trademark. Pemberton originally advertised his invention as a medicine, but it was soon apparent that more money was to be made in the drink market. The business was soon sold to Asa Candler, and later to the Woodruff family (both names you'll see on buildings around Atlanta).

4. When You Arrive

Only Chicago's O'Hare Airport has more traffic than Hartsfield.

Something else to experience in the airport: the contemporary art and photography hanging on the walls and the escalators—they're extra-long. Don't forget the people, either. This is an excellent place to observe the human race in all of its colorful, harried diversity.

There's a popular joke in the South that says when you die, regardless of whether you go to heaven or hell, you'll have to change planes in Atlanta. If you're arriving in Atlanta by air, you'll soon understand what the joke means. Look out your window as you come in for a landing. Planes to the left, planes to the right—you could be on the freeway. Hartsfield International Airport is the second-busiest airport in the world. It's also one of the few to have its own subway. Trains connect the five concourses and run every two minutes: an automated voice (like the ones in some supermarket checkout lines) tells you when they're coming and, once you're aboard, what stop you're at. Try to get a seat at the front of the lead car so you can watch the tunnel lights rushing at you.

Once out of the airport and in the car, you'll experience the freeways. Some go north and south, others go east and west, and I-285 circles the city. There are some impressive cloverleafs where these roads intersect and also some monumental traffic jams during rush hours. Still, most of the time they do make getting around faster, as intended.

Like many American cities, Atlanta grew in bursts and spurts over the years, along train lines and established roads. The result: there is no grid pattern to the streets (the way there is in Washington, D.C., or New York) except near downtown, and even there the exception is the rule. Some major thoroughfares are relatively straight; others meander like cowpaths. But it's not too hard to get the lay of the land. The city is divided into four geographic areas: Northeast (N.E.), Northwest (N.W.), Southeast (S.E.), and Southwest (S.W.). These areas merge downtown near the Five Points intersection (where Peachtree, Marietta, Decatur, Edgewood, and Whitehall streets come together), at the "Zero Milepost" in Underground Atlanta.

The only place you're likely to do a lot of walking is downtown, where things are relatively close together. Wear comfortable shoes; remember, you're dealing with hard city pavement. If

Like many big cities, Atlanta has a number of professional sports teams. The Atlanta/Fulton County Stadium (near the airport) is home to baseball's National League Braves as well as the NFL's Falcons. The Omni downtown is home turf for the NBA's Hawks. Georgia Tech and Georgia State University also stage sports events.

Check out the Peachtree Center MARTA station. The subway tunnel was blasted from solid granite, and the black rock walls have been left exposed. You can still see the marks where they put the explosives.

Like all Southern cities, Atlanta's economy was revolutionized by the introduction of mass air conditioning in the 1930s. This made it possible for people to work comfortably during the hot, humid, summer months.

you get tired, hop in a taxi. They're plentiful and not too expensive.

Other than your feet, the fastest way to get around is the Metropolitan Atlanta Rapid Transit Authority, or MARTA. We're talking subway here: the MARTA buses (they're white, with a blue, orange, and yellow diagonal stripe on the sides) go all over the place, but to use them you definitely need a map, and in most cases, a car is a more efficient and faster way to get around. The MARTA subway-monorail, however, is speedy, clean, and safe. It operates an east-west route from Avondale to Hightower and a north-south route from Chamblee to the airport. The fare is 85 cents to all points. If you have plans to visit anywhere outside of the metro area, or you're going to be in the city for any length of time, you'll save time and aggravation by renting a car.

In many ways, Atlanta resembles a giant suburb. True, there's a big-city downtown and pockets of high-rises here and there, but most of the city is made up of smaller buildings, apartments, and private homes. Shopping plazas pop up every ten blocks or so. Trees and parks are everywhere, and so are churches. The city gives you a sense of a place where real people live and work; in spite of its size and pace, it's a comfortable, rather than overwhelming, place to visit.

The weather is generally mild. Snow is rare (but not unheard of) in the winter. Spring brings azaleas, daffodils, and many other flowers: there's a weeklong Dogwood Festival every April to celebrate a city full of pink and white blossoms. Summer is hot and generally humid, while fall is mild and colorful with changing leaves. When-

ever you come, bring a raincoat; chances are you'll need it.

A lot of the things to do and see in Atlanta will be there whenever you come to visit. Others are seasonal, like the rides at Six Flags and theater at the Woodruff Center. Be sure and check the listings in local papers and magazines for stuff that's happening while you're there. You may luck into the experience of a lifetime!

*That green leafy vine you see everywhere is called **kudzu.** Introduced into this country from Japan over 100 years ago, it has taken over the South. In a single season a plant can grow as much as 100 feet.*

15

5. Downtown

You'll find the name "Peachtree" all over Atlanta, adorning everything from shopping centers to a road race. Peach trees, however, are not native to Georgia. Speculation is that the name derives from a long-ago corruption of "standing pitch tree," another name for pine tree.

he center of Atlanta, geographically, historically, and economically, is its downtown. Here is serious big-city razzle-dazzle. Huge hotels glisten in the sun, flanked by equally large office buildings and convention centers. Enclosed walkways arch overhead, connecting tower to tower in a futuristic network of protected passageways. Nestled in among the reflecting glass, steel, and concrete are other, older buildings with graceful large windows and carved granite doorways. Traffic surges through narrow streets; the sidewalks are crowded. There's a lot of energy in the air, and it's catching. You may find yourself walking faster than you usually do, just to keep up with the pace around you.

The Hotels

First, a word about atriums. The word was coined to describe the enclosed central courts in the houses of ancient Rome. Atriums have come a long way since then, due in large part to an Atlanta-based architect named John Portman who designed a number of the glitzy hotels here and in other big American cities.

Walk into the lobby of the **Hyatt Regency** and

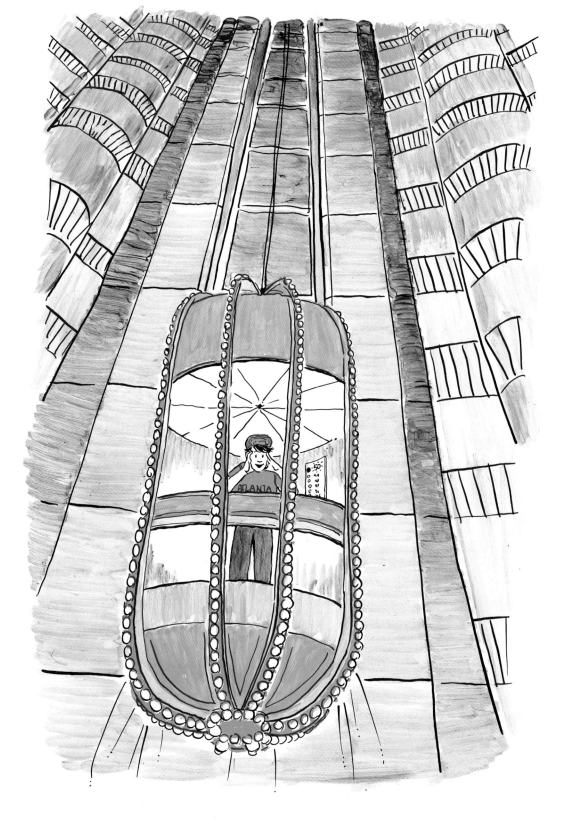

One revolution of the Polaris restaurant atop the Hyatt Regency takes about 45 minutes.

The Westin Peachtree Plaza Hotel has 1,074 rooms equipped with 1,100 alarm clocks, 1,400 "Do Not Disturb" signs, 38,772 towels, 2,197 mirrors, and 42,140 glass ashtrays. One hundred vacuum cleaners scour 125,475 square yards of carpet, which is enough to cover 35 football fields.

look up. The roof is 23 stories above you—you could fit a small skyscraper inside this building. Light-bedecked, pod-shaped glass elevators scurry up and down a massive black column, carrying guests to the rooms that ring each floor of the cavern. A stylized flower made of gold rods juts up a hundred feet from the floor. There are restaurants, trees, and music everywhere.

The Hyatt Regency, built in 1968, was the first Portman atrium hotel. It has a pool (of course) and a revolving restaurant on the roof. Taking the elevator up is an experience: you zoom up through the lobby and then burst through the roof, getting a bird's-eye view of the city before the blue-domed restaurant closes in on you. If you're afraid of heights, shut your eyes.

The view from atop the **Westin Peachtree Plaza** (which also has a revolving restaurant on the top floor) is even better than that from the Hyatt across the street, probably because the building is higher. This cylindrical gray-glass tower, another Portman design, is, at 723 feet, the world's tallest hotel. You can easily see Stone Mountain and other Atlanta landmarks from its summit. There used to be a half-acre lake in the lobby; now there is a forest of lighted pillars and chandeliers, so many that it can be a little difficult to find your way around. There's the obligatory pool, a health spa, and many shops and restaurants, all to keep the dazzled traveler happy.

The latest entry in the Portman hotel sweepstakes is the **Atlanta Marriott Marquis**, behind the Hyatt on Peachtree Center Avenue (it's the one with a roof that looks a little like a washing machine agitator). Here the interior atrium soars

50 stories, and two of the glass-pod elevators travel 1,000 feet per minute, fast enough to leave your stomach behind on the floor below. There are, of course, trees, art, restaurants, and shops, and a huge ribbonlike sculpture to help fill some of the 9 million cubic feet of space under the skylighted roof.

These three hotels are part of a 10-acre business and lodging complex called **Peachtree Center**. Other stuff here: an underground mall with shops and restaurants, office towers, and two huge buildings that house the **Apparel Mart** and the **Merchandise Mart**, which have showrooms where, if you're a retailer, you can buy goods wholesale.

The Omni/CNN Tour/Georgia World Congress
Just a few blocks to the west of the towers on Peachtree Street is the **CNN Center** (formerly the Omni), another atrium building that houses the Omni Hotel, two 14-story office buildings, and Turner Broadcasting Systems' two 24-hour news divisions, Cable News Network and Headline News. Next door is the Omni Coliseum, home of the NBA Hawks and also the setting for circuses, ice shows, horse shows, and other indoor attractions. The huge building across the street is the **Georgia World Congress**, convention center extraordinaire.

Take a stroll around the floor of CNN Center.

In 1988 the Omni Coliseum was the site of the Democratic National Convention.

For a distinct change of pace, old-fashioned horse-drawn carriage rides are available outside the Peachtree Plaza. Ask the concierge for information.

A glass roof arches high above you. High-tech white girders are everywhere. There are places to get fast food and a store featuring merchandise from various branches of the Turner Empire, including the ruby red slippers from *The Wizard of Oz*.

If you're at all interested in broadcast news, the **CNN Studio Tour** is well worth your time. It starts with a spectacular 8-story escalator ride up through the center of the atrium. On the balcony at the top are exhibits that chronicle the rise of Turner Broadcasting and detail its various divisions. Then your guide leads you on a winding route of corridors and stairs, past offices and stacks of videotapes, to an overlook of the CNN newsroom and studio. Television monitors and computer terminals are everywhere. Writers, producers, and technicians bustle around, conferring with each other and talking on the phone. In the background, all lit up, is the studio where the actual broadcast (you can see it on some of the monitors) originates.

All in all, it's pretty exciting. You half expect to see William Hurt or Holly Hunter come bursting in with a breaking story, the way they did in the movie *Broadcast News*. Well, they won't, but you may catch a glimpse of news anchors you recognize. The guides are very good at describing just how a story gets from where it's happening to this room and from the studio to the television in your home and are happy to answer any questions you might have.

Then on through more corridors, past more offices and control rooms (you wonder how these workers feel, having people looking in at them all day) to the Headline News newsroom and studio, basically a smaller version of what's upstairs. When you finally emerge onto the floor of the atrium again, you've had a taste of what TV news is like—fast-paced, claustrophobic (these guys almost never see the sun except on a monitor), and rarely dull.

Underground Atlanta

Near Five Points in the heart of downtown, here is a 12-acre "underground city," formed in the early twentieth century when the City of Atlanta built a series of bridges over the railroad tracks, in the process raising the level of many streets. The old shopfronts below were abandoned until the early 1960s, when they were

Coming soon to Underground Atlanta: a pavilion dedicated to the city's native drink, Coca-Cola, plus a collection of history exhibits called Atlanta Heritage Row.

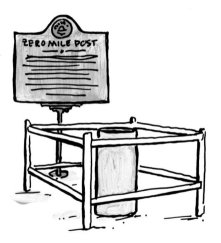

When the Zero Milepost was erected in 1850, it marked the center of a circular city that extended one mile in every direction. Today Metro Atlanta covers 4,326 square miles.

rediscovered and converted into a popular entertainment center called Underground Atlanta.

A second wave of renovation has just ended, and Underground Atlanta has been gentrified. Like a lot of places in the city, it's geared to tourists and the consumer dollar, but it also offers a glimpse of what the business district of the city used to be like before the era of steel rebar and concrete. The Zero Mile Marker is here, a simple stone that stands close to the site of the original Western and Atlantic Railroad stake that marked the birth of the city as well as its geographic center. Here, too, along with fountains, waterfalls, trendy shops and restaurants, and a 138-foot light tower, are turn-of-the-century buildings and brick streets. The restored Georgia Railroad Freight Depot, built in 1869 and the oldest standing building in Atlanta, is now the home of the **New Georgia Railway**, where on any Saturday you can board an old steam train on a trip around Atlanta or out to Stone Mountain Park. It's a great way to spend a few hours; grab some peanuts from the snack bar and settle back. The landscape is a little different from what it was 50 or 100 years ago, but remember as you watch the city roll by that many people first saw it from a railroad car, and trains were the reason for the city's founding.

SCITREK

Hands down, the most exciting indoor space in town. The brand-new **Science and Technology Museum of Atlanta**, or **SCITREK** for short, resembles nothing so much as a huge, classy video arcade, with "hands-on" physical science exhibits taking the place of Pac-Man and electronic race cars. The big hall is dark, with bright lights in primary colors everywhere, super-graphics on the walls, and black girders overhead. There's a hum of excitement as you enter. Kids dart to and fro, calling to one another, "Hey, come over here! Try this!" You may think you dislike science, but chances are you'll revise your opinion after a visit here. This isn't science the way it's often taught, a welter of equations and dry facts. This is FUN!

The museum is divided into four main areas: Electricity and Magnetism, Light and Perception, Simple Machines, and Kidspace. The exhibits all have explanatory panels that tell you what to do, what's happening as you do it, and additional facts that you might find interesting. Generate electricity by pedaling a bicycle: different bulbs light up, depending on how fast you go. Take a picture of your shadow (really), or lift a 500-pound automobile engine with a pulley. The magnetic repulsion exhibit sends a metal ring shooting skyward when you push a button (it makes a very satisfying 'whomp' sound as well), while the Van de Graaf generator will make your hair stand on end—literally. And that's just the beginning of what's here. It's a science circus, worth visit after visit.

Kidspace is an area for younger kids, ages 2-7, but it's well worth checking out. There's a closed circuit TV here that you can program yourself, plus face paints, a big waterworks table, and various kinds of music generators. And don't miss the gift shop; there are all kinds of wonderful toys, books, and gadgets for sale. It's a good place to do some serious shopping, or to have someone do some for you. Drop a hint to your parents.

SCITREK also has a hall for temporary exhibits. One recent display, "The Science of Sports," featured trained rats named Larry Byrd and Dr. J in a game of slam-dunk basketball.

There's another Flatiron Building in New York City. It's more famous, but Atlanta's was built five years earlier.

Other Stuff Downtown

Part of the fun of a big city is just walking around, looking at people and soaking up atmosphere. **Woodruff Park**, on Peachtree in the center of downtown, is a good place to start. It's a summer haven for lunch-munchers and open-air preachers urging you to be saved. Right next to it, at 84 Peachtree Street, is the baby blue-trimmed **Flatiron Building**, Atlanta's oldest standing skyscraper. Named for its narrow, triangular shape, it's home to the **Atlanta Preservation Center**, which sponsors walking tours of some of the city's neighborhoods.

The Flatiron Building is on the edge of the **Fairlie-Poplar** district, named for two of its streets and home to many of downtown Atlanta's finest older buildings. The **Candler Building** (127 Peachtree Street), built in 1906, is a good example. Built for Coca-Cola magnate Asa Candler, it has long been an Atlanta landmark. Check out the lavish carvings over the windows: many have recognizable historical figures in them, symbolizing various artistic and scientific themes.

Just up Peachtree from Woodruff Park is the red granite **Georgia-Pacific Center**, home to the downtown branch of Atlanta's High Museum of Art. The museum is reached through the lobby of the office building, which is dominated by a huge Louise Nevelson sculpture that resembles a forest of abstract white totem poles. The museum itself is on three levels, connected by a sloping wood walkway (there are elevators, too). The galleries are light and quiet, a pleasant refuge from the street outside; the art can be anything from classical to the newest of the new.

6. Near Downtown

The eastern part of Inman Park was the site of the fiercest fighting of the Battle of Atlanta on July 22, 1864.

There's a lot of stuff to see in Atlanta that's near downtown but not really within walking distance unless you're into serious hiking. Some sights are reachable by MARTA; for others, you need a car.

Neighborhoods
Like any city, Atlanta has them, though to the uninitiated they may seem rather hard to find. The most obvious neighborhood is downtown, easily identified by its skyline. Almost in the shadow of the big buildings is **Auburn Avenue** and the **Martin Luther King Historical District**—more about them in a bit. Two miles east of downtown is **Inman Park**, a beautiful area of big Victorian homes grouped around a small park of the same name. Many of these storybook mansions (most have turrets, gables, balconies, and fancy molding worthy of a fairy tale) are being restored, and this area is currently a very trendy place to live. Look for the yellow and black butterfly banner in many windows: it's the symbol of the neighborhood.

Close by Inman Park is **Little Five Points**. It's definitely on the funky side, with vintage clothing stores and boutiques that cater to new wave

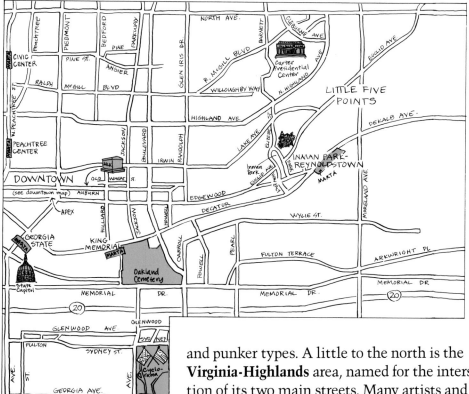

*Inman Park was Atlanta's first planned suburb. The area was developed in the 1880s and connected to downtown by a five-minute streetcar ride. You can still see the old green and rust-colored **Trolley Barn**, built in 1889, at 501 Edgewood Avenue.*

and punker types. A little to the north is the **Virginia-Highlands** area, named for the intersection of its two main streets. Many artists and professional people live here. The neighborhood offers restaurants, taverns, and offbeat shops; on weekends it's crowded and lively.

Another distinct neighborhood is **Midtown**, with its theaters, museums, and office buildings (more about that, too, later). Nearby is **Ansley Park**, another enclave of majestic homes, winding streets, and greenery, and **Morningside** (more of the same). Other notable neighborhoods include **Druid Hills**, developed in the early twentieth century by Joel Hurt, the same man responsible for Inman Park, and designed by Frederick Law Olmsted, the man who designed New York City's Central Park. Here are more big homes and landscaped lawns. One house worth seeing is **Callanwolde**, built in 1920 with Coca-Cola money and now the Fine Arts Center for DeKalb County.

To the west of downtown is the neighborhood known as the **West End**, one of Atlanta's first commuter neighborhoods. Noteworthy here is the Victorian **Wren's Nest** on Gordon Street, once the home of author Joel Harris, creator of the "Uncle Remus" stories. It contains, among other things, a diorama from Walt Disney's *Song of the South*.

The State Capitol

Massive and cross-shaped, with the largest gold dome in the United States, this nineteenth-century edifice is a treasure trove of Georgia history. Guided tours are available; they're short and well worth taking if you want to learn all sorts of interesting facts about the place. Case in point: bet you didn't know this building (it's Indiana limestone on the outside and Georgia marble on the inside) weighed over 70,000 tons (that's about 15,680,000 pounds)? Definitely heavy.

The central rotunda is 237 feet high from floor to ceiling and ringed with old paintings and statues. The northern and southern ends of the buildings are atriums four stories high (could they have been the inspiration for John Portman's hotels?) hung with old Georgian and Confederate flags. On the fourth floor is a nifty natural history museum that's definitely worth a visit. Here are dioramas of Georgia wildlife and history, cases of crystals, fish, snakes, a stuffed buffalo, Indian artifacts, and an impressive collection of pistols and rifles.

Don't forget, this is a working state capitol. The governor's office is on the main floor; you

The Capitol dome is covered with 60 ounces of 23-carat gold leaf that's as thin as tissue paper. If compressed, it would be about the size of a softball.

Built in 1889, the State Capitol came in $118.43 under its budget of $1 million. Today the building is worth about $230 million.

27

can peek through the glass door and see people busy at their desks. If the legislature is in session, the marble halls are abuzz with activity. Proceedings in both the House and the Senate can be viewed from the visitor's galleries on the fourth floor, but don't expect to see anything momentous happening. Government in general is not a spectator sport.

The gardens that surround the Capitol are full of statues and historical plaques. A good place to rest your legs and improve your mind.

Zoo Atlanta/Atlanta Cyclorama

Located in Grant Park (a nice place for a walk or jog all by itself), **Zoo Atlanta** is in the middle of a massive face-lift. Construction is everywhere; signs announce attractions to come. But even in flux, this is a zoo well worth a visit. It's small, so you can explore the whole place thoroughly in an hour or two without experiencing animal overload.

Flamingos greet you just inside the gate. Next is the elephant house, where the big pachyderms make their home, and then on to the Ford African Rain Forest, where you can watch three families of silver lowland gorillas prowl a hilly habitat (modeled after their home in the wild) and bask in the sun. Nearby, yellow Sumatran orangutans scamper up and down a big, rope-festooned climbing tree. There's also a soaring net cage full of birds—you can walk inside and pretend you're in an African forest—plus a wildlife theater for viewing nature films. Opening in 1989 is Masai Mara, an African plains exhibit that will be home to lions, zebras, giraffes, and rhinos. Other "habitats" in the works include

Mzima Springs, an African watering hole; South American jungle; and Arctic seashore.

The reptile building offers a glimpse of what the zoo used to be like; it's old and dark, with not much room for the animals to move around in. However, there's an excellent assortment of snakes, spiders, lizards, and turtles here— let's hope they get a better home in the future. Other attractions: bears, sea lions, and a children's zoo with sheep, llamas, pigs, and other animals you can touch. Take a ride on the zoo train that chugs every day in the summer, weekends the rest of the year; it's only 75 cents. And check out the gift shop for an assortment of animal-related books, toys, and zoo memorabilia.

Right next to the zoo is the Atlanta **Cyclo-rama**, a huge circular painting and diorama of the Battle of Atlanta housed in the big gray building across from the zoo's visitor's center. The only way to see it is to take the guided tour, but if you have an extra half-hour and are even slightly interested in the Civil War, it's thirty minutes well spent. First you view a short film, then walk through a tunnel to a revolving plat-form in the middle of the painting. The platform rotates twice completely as you sit there. During the first revolution, there's music, lighting effects, and a taped narration that explains what the painting depicts. During the second, your guide will give you some facts about the paint-ing itself.

What you see: a 42-foot-high, 358-foot-long work of art, painted in 1885-86, that depicts the Civil War battle that resulted in the destruction of Atlanta and, more important, turned the course of the Civil War definitively against the

The "Vanishing Animal" stickers on some cages mean that these creatures are disappearing in the wild.

Also in the Cyclorama building: the old steam engine "Texas," a museum, and a very good Civil War bookstore.

One of the fallen figures on the foreground diorama has the face of Clark Gable as Rhett Butler in Gone With the Wind. *The likeness was added after Gable himself suggested it.*

Confederacy. Troops mass before your eyes; fighting stretches to the horizon, and the sky is filled with the smoke of battle. The action extends to the 3-D diorama in the foreground, added fifty years after the painting was finished. Soldiers grapple with one another; some lie dead and dying in the red Georgia clay among cannon, wagons, and broken railroad tracks. Both the painting and the foreground figures are very realistic, and together they give you a visceral feel for what war was like a hundred plus years ago. There are no tanks in this painting, no airplanes or missiles—if the soldiers aren't walking, they're on horseback. One thing hasn't changed, though, and never will: the suffering and loss of life incurred in a conflict of this magnitude. Looking at the pain and carnage depicted in this painting makes you wonder if war is ever worth the human price it demands.

Martin Luther King, Jr., Memorial and Historical Site/Sweet Auburn District/APEX Museum
To the east of Atlanta's central business district lies **Auburn Avenue**, a street that in many ways symbolizes the spiritual and economic heart of the city's black community. After the Civil War, many former slaves bought property along what was then called Wheat Street (the name was changed in 1893 to the more stylish-sounding Auburn). Over the years a prosperous community grew up, with black-owned banks, insurance companies, markets, and professional offices as well as many churches and nightclubs. The vitality of life here, as well as the opportunities available for Afro-Americans, prompted political leader John Wesley Dobbs to dub the district "Sweet Auburn" in the 1930s. It was also

here, on a January morning in 1929, that Martin Luther King, Jr., the civil rights leader and Auburn Avenue's most famous resident, was born, and it is here that he lies buried.

The **Martin Luther King, Jr., Birth Home**, built in 1895, is a handsome two-story structure that bears witness to the prosperity of the neighborhood during the first part of the twentieth century (though it seems humble in comparison to some of the mansions in Inman Park and Midtown). A half-block away stands the **Martin Luther King, Jr., Center for Nonviolent Social Change, Inc.**, a striking modern office complex. This is home to an organization founded by Dr. King's widow, Coretta Scott King, which seeks to further her husband's dreams of economic and social equality for all people, no matter what their color. Here, too, are exhibits on King's life and work; Freedom Hall, a conference and cultural center; and King's grave.

The tomb, a simple raised rectangle of white marble, stands alone in the middle of a five-tiered reflecting pool with fountains and flags at one end. Engraved on the stone are the words of an old Negro spiritual, words that ended Dr. King's famous "I have a Dream" speech, given at the Lincoln Memorial during the 1963 March on Washington: "Free at last, free at last, thank God Almighty, we're free at last!" There is little sound, save for the murmur of passing traffic and the gurgle of water from the fountains, but the silence is as eloquent as the man himself was in life.

Martin Luther King, Jr., was only thirty-nine when he was gunned down by an assassin in Memphis, Tennessee. During his short life he led millions of people, black and white, in a

The Atlanta Daily World, *founded in 1928, was the country's first daily newspaper published by and for blacks; today, it's the oldest.*

nonviolent campaign for racial equality that changed forever the pattern of segregation in this country. His passionate actions and writings on behalf of human and civil rights earned him, at the age of 35, the Nobel Peace Prize. Here, in the middle of city bustle, is a quiet place that honors his memory. The white sarcophagus stands as a reminder of a courage and devotion to principle that we all can aspire to.

Near the Center for Nonviolent Social Change are several churches with prominent places in Atlanta history. The **Ebenezer Baptist Church** was where Martin Luther King, Jr., and his father and grandfather before him, preached. The **Wheat Street Baptist Church** (365 Auburn) and the **Big Bethel African Methodist Episcopal Church** (220 Auburn) testify by size alone to the traditional importance of the church in black society.

Further along the street toward downtown lies the **APEX**, or **African American Panoramic**

The Ebenezer Baptist Church has seen its share of King-related tragedy. It was here, in 1968, that Dr. King's funeral was held, and here, six years later, that his mother was killed by a gunman as she sat at the organ.

Experience. This museum, housed in the handsomely restored red brick warehouselike John Wesley Dobbs building, contains several exhibits on the history of Auburn Avenue. A corner drugstore, circa 1920, has been re-created, and you can sit in an old trolley car and watch a video called "Sweet Auburn: Street of Pride." Also here: African textiles, wonderful wooden masks and sculptures, and artifacts from black history.

The Carter Library

On a thirty-acre hillside site east of downtown (the second-highest point in the city) sits the Carter Presidential Center, four interconnected, graceful gray buildings that house the office of our former chief executive, his presidential papers, and various nonprofit organizations that he sponsors. **The Museum of the Jimmy Carter Library** chronicles Carter's life, his campaign for our nation's highest office, and the achievements of his administration (1977-1980), as well as offering insights into the presidency as an institution.

Sound dull? Well, it's not. In the Town Meeting section you can ask the president a question via video monitor and get a taped answer; in another section you can choose your own response to a terrorist crisis and find out what your course of action would result in. There are videos and films galore, as well as all sorts of interesting odds and ends: gifts the Carters received while in office, campaign paraphernalia, and more. There's an exact replica of the Oval Office as it was during the Carter presidency, with a taped description by the former president: a rare glimpse of a place you've certainly heard a lot about. The floor-to-ceiling

The row of small houses across the street from King's birthplace, built in 1905 to house textile workers and now awaiting restoration, were known as "shotgun" houses because, theoretically, a bullet entering the front door could exit through the similarly aligned back door. The contrast between these humble dwellings and the high-rise skyline to the west offers a capsule lesson in big-city economic diversity.

On the grounds: a serenely lovely Japanese garden next to a small lake, with benches nearby to sit and admire the great view of the downtown skyline. There's also a restaurant in the main building where you can get lunch.

The highest hill in Atlanta is crowned by Macy's Department Store, just south of Peachtree Plaza in the heart of the downtown business district.

windows look out on a spring-blooming rose garden; the original "The Buck Stops Here" sign (from Harry Truman) sits atop the chief executive's desk. With a little imagination, you could be indoors at 1600 Pennsylvania Avenue, privy to all kinds of important goings-on.

Oh, one more thing. Don't forget to take a good look at the glass wall that looks in on the library itself. Here are stored over 27 million documents, video- and audiotapes, pictures, and reels of motion-picture film pertaining to the policies and activities of the presidency and executive office during four short years. That's definitely enough material to keep the researchers and historians who use the library busy for a long time, and it gives you an idea of the mind-boggling scope of governmental bureaucracy in the twentieth century.

Also of Interest near Downtown

Oakland Cemetery, just north of Grant Park, is the oldest cemetery in Atlanta. Founded in 1850, its leafy avenues are crammed with ornate funeral statuary; until 1884, nearly every person who died in Atlanta was buried here. Occupants include Union and Confederate soldiers, *Gone With the Wind* author Margaret Mitchell, and grand slam golfer Bobby Jones.

To the west of downtown is the **Herndon House**, home of one of Atlanta's most prosperous black businessmen. Born a slave and founder of Atlanta Life Insurance Company, Alonzo Herndon built this mansion in 1910—a sumptuous example of black achievement.

7. Midtown

Albuquerque Academy
MIDDLE SCHOOL LIBRARY
6400 Wyoming Blvd. N.E.
Albuquerque, NM 87109

bout two miles to the north of downtown, along Peachtree, is the area called Midtown. In the 1960s, Midtown was Atlanta's hippie district; today the big, tree-shaded houses near 15th Street and Piedmont Park are worth hundreds of thousands of dollars.

Fox Theatre

About halfway between downtown and Midtown on Peachtree and one of Atlanta's more unique landmarks. Built in 1929 and originally intended as a temple for a 5,000-member chapter of the

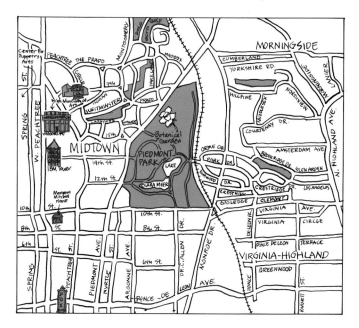

Shriners, this huge Moorish/Egyptian/Art Deco palace was converted early in its history to a movie theater and concert hall. Today, it showcases films, specialty acts, rock concerts, plays, and musicals. Attending a show here is one way to see the building; another is to take one of the Atlanta Preservation Center's walking tours. However you manage to get inside, you're bound to be amazed by the opulence, extravagance, and sheer lunatic scope of what you see around you.

The outside of the building, with its minarets and onion domes, give you a hint of what lurks inside. The arched, mosaic-festooned main lobby intensifies the Arabian Nights mood, but nothing prepares you for the mind-boggling main auditorium. The 64,000 square feet of floor space (a good-sized house is only about 2,500 square feet), capable of seating more than 4,000 people, is designed as the courtyard of a medieval Moorish castle. Crenellated walls with parapets and turrets run from the edges of the stage to the upper balconies. Above you arches a deep blue night sky atwinkle with stars and broken by drifting clouds. The stage itself is, at 140 feet, one of the longest ever built, and the proscenium arch 80 feet above it is crowned with what looks like a walkway lit by old-fashioned streetlights. Ornate grilles, stage curtains bedecked with mosques and men on horseback, and overhead striped canopies complete the otherworldly, fairy-tale effect.

The rest of the building has a similar mood. Middle Eastern motifs are everywhere: arches, scarabs, and intricate Arabic designs on virtually every available surface. The tomb of the Egyptian Pharoah Tutankhamen was discovered a few

The Fox's Moller organ, one of the largest theater organs in the country, has 3,610 pipes.

The Fox was almost torn down in the mid-1970s to make way for a skyscraper, but a preservation campaign organized by concerned citizens managed to save it.

years before the Fox was built, and the subsequent craze for all things Egyptian is amply reflected in the architecture and decorative detailing of the building. If your gender permits, by all means check out the ladies' lounge on the mezzanine—with its bas-reliefs, hieroglyphics, and throne chairs, it's like no other bathroom you're likely to experience!

Varsity Diner
Just west of the Fox and across from Georgia Tech stands an extravaganza of a different order.

Often billed as the world's largest drive-in restaurant, the orange and yellow tiled **Varsity Diner** (it looks the way a diner ought to look, functional and a little funky) is actually best experienced from the inside. You stand in line at what could be the world's longest counter and place your order with any one of more than ten hash-slingers in red Varsity hats (headwear available at the gift shop behind you). The fare here is strictly chili-dogs, onion rings, and peach pie, but what did you expect?

Woodruff Arts Center/High Museum

The tone of the neighborhood gets more highbrow as you move uptown. Here are classy business and retail centers like **Colony Square**, distinctive towers like the **IBM building** (the tallest building around and the one with the old-fashioned-looking pitched roof), theaters, and museums. The imposing, white stone **Woodruff Arts Center** offers a variety of entertainment options. Here you can catch a concert by the **Atlanta Symphony Orchestra** in the 1,800-seat Symphony Hall, or see a play or musical (recent offerings include *Peter Pan* and *Amadeus*) in either the **Alliance Theatre** or its smaller sibling, the **Studio Theatre**. The Woodruff is also home to the **Atlanta College of Art** and the **Atlanta Children's Theatre**, which offers biannual productions of classics such as *Treasure Island* and *Beauty and the Beast*.

Next door, the **High Museum of Art** (it's part of the same complex) is a work of art all by itself. Designed by architect Richard Meier and built in 1983, the gleaming white building sits on a slight rise back from the street, its curves,

This is a great place to experience art. The whiteness of the building is like a blank canvas against which the paintings, sculpture, and other objects are shown to maximum effect. Plus the building itself is fun; light and airy, full of beams and glass, it's designed to stimulate your senses and keep you moving. There's an area on the lower level that's just for little kids—of interest even for bigger types. And, like many museums, this one has an outstanding gift shop.

The museum also hosts many traveling exhibitions every year, so there's always a variety of things to see.

The Center also has a 300-seat theater where performances are given, a school that conducts workshops for those interested in making and working with their own figures, and a store with puppet-connected items. Every summer there's a six-week Summer Festival, with productions by different puppet companies.

angles, and windows complemented by a big, colorful Alexander Calder stabile sculpture on the lawn. Inside is a four-story, naturally lit atrium (yes, another one) shaped like a quarter of a pie, with galleries on two sides and a wall of windows on the curved third.

Take the elevator to the top floor; a walkway descends the height of the atrium, running switchback along the window wall. A horse made of crumpled metal greets you as you step off the lift. Nearby is Marilyn Monroe as interpreted by Andy Warhol—the familiar face is multiplied eight times and colored Day-Glo shades of fuschia, yellow, turquoise, and orange. Other highlights of the museum's permanent collection include European paintings from the Renaissance to the nineteenth century, beautiful Gallé carved glass vases from the turn of the century, African masks and wooden sculpture, and some great Art Deco.

Center for Puppetry Arts
Round the corner from the High Museum in an old red brick schoolhouse, the center was established in 1978 (Kermit the Frog, accompanied by his creator Jim Henson, cut the ceremonial ribbon) and houses the largest private collection of puppets in the country. Among the 400-plus figures here (not all are on display at once) are pre-Columbian clay puppets, two-dimensional shadow figures from France, a brick in a skirt (yes, it's a puppet, too), and elaborate marionettes as well as Muppets and some of the elaborate Henson figures from such films as *The Dark Crystal* and *Labyrinth*. There's also a 15-minute videotape, "Through the Looking

Glass," which gives you some interesting background on the history and practice of puppetry arts.

Atlanta Botanical Garden

A great place to go for a stroll, sit in the sun, or admire some flowers. The 60-acre garden has fountains, wooden benches, wooded trails, and a lovely rose garden. There's a small gift shop and some ivy-covered topiary animals—an elephant with raised trunk by the woods, a dragon by the parking lot and another in the Lotus Pond in front of the spectacular Dorothy Champman Fuqua Conservatory (the dragons are on loan).

This brand-new, 16,000-square-foot building boasts four exhibit areas: a rotunda that houses tropical plants, a desert area and Mediterranean house, a special exhibit area, and an orangerie. In the rotunda, the air is warm and misty. The sound of a 14-foot waterfall drowns out that of distant traffic. Palm trees tower above you, and lush tropical vegetation crowds next to the walkways. The desert and Mediterranean area next door is home to cacti and other plants from South America, Madagascar, and California, while the orangerie has a number of plants, such as coffee and mangos, that are of historical economic importance.

The Botanical Garden is situated at the northern end of **Piedmont Park**, Atlanta's best-known and biggest green space. A good place for a jog, a picnic lunch, or an outdoor break from all the sightseeing you've been doing.

Signs placed throughout the conservatory describe the plants and their natural habitats. Unfortunately, many of them are now endangered species. One of the stated aims of this new exhibit is to make people aware of the fragile state of the plant world. Let's hope it succeeds!

How to make a topiary animal: construct a frame out of heavy metal wire, stuff it with special moss, and then plant ivy in the moss. Water regularly.

8. Buckhead

Legend has it that the area's name came from a deer's head that hung in a local tavern.

bout three miles north of downtown and one of Atlanta's ritziest addresses, Buckhead began life as a stagecoach stop in the 1840s and has come a long way since. Here are many beautiful private homes; here also, some of Atlanta's best shopping (and in a city crammed with places where you can drop your dollars, that's saying something!).

A good way to get a taste of the neighborhood is to take a leisurely drive along **West Paces Ferry Road**. Here, set back from the street by sweeping, artfully landscaped lawns and sheltered by huge trees, are some of the biggest, fanciest houses you're likely to see anywhere. The **Governor's Mansion**, sitting on 18 acres behind iron gates, may be the biggest, but it's by no means the best-looking.

Does looking at the outside of these mansions make you want to peek inside one? Then wend your way to the **Atlanta Historical Society** nearby. Here stands the **Swan House**, an elaborate Palladian villa set in the midst of 22 beautiful acres of woods and gardens.

This place is as grand inside as you might imagine. The rooms are large, light, and sumptuously

furnished with antiques and art. Chandeliers, elaborate molding, and beautiful carpets are everywhere. The Inman family, who owned the house, had small children when they moved in. What fun those children must have had sliding down the banisters of the sweeping staircase in the front hall (though it's high enough that maybe their mother didn't let them)!

A word of warning: the only way you are allowed to see the Swan House is to take the tour. The guides, members of the Atlanta Historical Society, have the best of intentions, but often they ramble on endlessly, telling you lots of stuff you probably don't want to hear. If you have the patience for this, stick it out. If not, try

Built in 1928, the Swan House takes its name from its mistress's fondness for the graceful, cantankerous birds. Their image appears throughout the house as a decorative motif.

If you're itching for a walk, the Swan Woods Trail offers a lovely meander through the forest.

The Tullie Smith house was originally the center of an 800-acre farm. Note the "parson's room" off the front porch, where traveling preachers could put up for the night without awakening the family.

to get a glimpse of the front hall through the front door: you'll get the idea.

Also on the Historical Society grounds: the **Tullie Smith House**, an 1840s plantation house moved here from DeKalb County in 1969. Together with its barn and collection of out-buildings (also moved from elsewhere), it shows how a middle-class Georgia farm family lived and worked in the mid-nineteenth century. A tour is required here as well; the same warning applies.

A Word about Shopping

There's a lot to buy in Atlanta. The city is dotted with shopping plazas and ringed with malls—twenty-two, to be exact, of which eight qualify as "super" malls. Add to this countless specialty shops tucked away on every other side street, and you've got a consumer's paradise. You may ask, "Who needs all this stuff?" And you'd definitely have a point. However, chances are once inside a Toys-R-Us or a Neiman-Marcus, you'll forget about need (we're way beyond basic food, shelter, and clothing here) and just revel in the sheer variety of options for your dollar.

Of all Atlanta neighborhoods, Buckhead most qualifies as Mecca for shop-aholics. Here is the exclusive **Phipps Plaza**, home to Saks, Lord and Taylor, and sixty other stores. Across the street sprawls huge **Lenox Square** mall, a miniature city featuring Neiman-Marcus, Macy's, Rich's, Banana Republic, The Limited, The Gap, and 200-plus other shops. Here you can catch a fashion show in one of the mall's "streets," eat gourmet chocolate while people-watching, browse in a bookstore, or check out the latest in electronic toys. The options are mind-boggling.

9. Decatur

ix miles east of downtown, this area is actually a town distinct from the city around it. Built where two old Indian trails came together, Decatur boasts many old buildings and a historic town square.

Fernbank Science Center and Forest

Located on a quiet side street, this 65-acre woodland and museum complex serves as the science center for the DeKalb County school system, so chances are that when you visit there will be a lot of other kids here, too. The main building houses a number of natural history and science exhibits, many of them "hands-on." Here you can make a tornado appear in a cylinder of water by pressing a button, watch a radar display in a weather exhibit, or peer inside an actual Apollo 6 space capsule.

Absolutely not to be missed: a show in the center's planetarium, one of the nation's largest. Take a seat inside the 500-seat theater and marvel as the starry universe is re-created above your head.

The woodland that surrounds the center is "old-growth" forest, meaning that no one has ever farmed or logged it, and it is substantially as it was hundreds of years ago. A two-mile paved trail winds through the woods. Just think: all of

Fernbank also has an observatory with a 36-inch reflecting telescope; on some nights, weather permitting, you can use it to look at real stars.

That funny-looking object in the center of the planetarium floor (the one that looks like a black satellite on stilts) is the Zeiss Mark V star projector responsible for creating what you see above you. It can project 9,000 stars, weighs 2½ tons, and contains six miles of wiring.

Atlanta, with its busy freeways and towering office buildings, was like this quiet, leafy glen just a hundred and fifty years ago.

Coming in 1991: the **Fernbank Museum of Natural History**, to be located on 25 acres at the edge of the Fernbank Forest in Druid Hills. Advance reports indicate it will be big (150,000 square feet) and chock-full of great, "hands-on" exhibits. The center of the museum will be a "Walk Through Time in Georgia," which will take visitors on an animated sight and sound journey from the beginning of the universe to the present. Also here will be a Naturalist Center, with all kinds of scientific equipment you can use, plus a Discovery Room (shaped like the State of Georgia) where you can slide down the Chattahoochee River, squish through the Okefenokee Swamp, and look for fossils and rocks. Next to the Discovery Room is planned the Fantasy Forest, where you'll be able to experience (among other things) how a cat sees at night and what it's like to have raccoon paws instead of hands.

Emory University

Actually not in Decatur, but nearby Druid Hills. Founded in 1836, the university moved to its present 500-acre campus in the early twentieth century; today it has over 8,000 students.

To visit: the **Emory University Museum of Art and Archaeology**, in Michael C. Carlos Hall on the University Quadrangle. The museum is small but extremely elegant, with all sorts of artifacts from the Near East and classical Greece and Rome as well as items from ancient Mexico and Central America. Of special interest: the golden Egyptian mummy cases and an actual mummy dating from 300 B.C.

Another big attraction will be an IMAX theater with a three-story-high screen. Watching a movie here will be a whole-body experience—you'll feel as if you're actually in the picture!

*Also of interest at Emory, though it's not geared for visitors: the **Centers for Disease Control**, notable for AIDS research (it also deals with issues of health safety, disease prevention, and education).*

10. Attractions Outside the City

nterstate 285, otherwise known as the Perimeter Highway, makes a big ring around the city. Outside this circle are a number of places worth visiting.

Stone Mountain Park
Located sixteen miles east of Atlanta on Highway 78 and named for the huge curved gray stone

in its middle, Stone Mountain is the largest mass of exposed granite in the world. This 300-million-year-old geological wonder stands 825 feet above the surrounding piedmont, measures 5 miles around, and covers 583 acres. Want to climb it? Start at the railroad depot at the west entrance of the park. After about 40 minutes of energetic scrambling over lichen- and moss-encrusted rock, you're at the top, with a spectacular view in every direction. Confederate flags flap above your head (this is a good place to fly a kite). Grab a drink from the concession stand and explore. After a rainstorm there are often standing pools of water with small fairy shrimp (yes, shrimp) in them, plus all kinds of other interesting plant and bird life. Also here: the **Theater in the Sky Movie House**, which shows a film about the mountain.

On the north face is carved the **Confederate Memorial**, with huge figures of Confederate President Jefferson Davis and Southern Generals Robert E. Lee and Stonewall Jackson riding on horseback 400 feet above the ground. Every evening in summer there's a spectacular rock-and-roll laser show given on the Memorial Hall lawn in front of the carving. Bring a picnic and a blanket, then curl up and watch huge light figures cavort in the air above you, their antics followed by a very satisfying fireworks display.

The park's 3,200 acres offer all kinds of things to do. Some options: take a 30-minute, old-fashioned train ride around the base of the mountain or a cable-car ride from near the laser-viewing lawn to the top of the peak. There are several large lakes here that boast water slides, beaches, cruises on an old paddlewheeler, and boat rentals. You can fish, ice-skate, play golf or

The carving was begun in 1923 and discontinued in 1928. Work was resumed in 1964, and the work was finished in 1970.

The carving is 90 feet tall and 190 feet wide. It stands 11½ feet out from the side of the mountain. The sculptor who started it later created the massive figures on Mt. Rushmore in South Dakota.

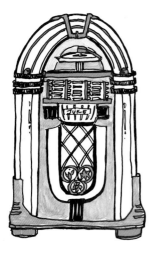

tennis, hike, run around a playground, or camp overnight. If you're feeling quiet, feed the ducks and swans near the riverboat complex, or listen to a bell concert by the park's **carillon** (the swooping black-ribbed structure on the edge of the lake which looks like a bird about to take flight).

Wait, there's more. The **Antebellum Plantation** offers a collection of buildings (relocated from elsewhere) that represent a pre-Civil War Georgia plantation. Here is everything from slave cabins to a very fancy 1840s manor house. The green, tree-shaded setting, though a little artificial, is very pleasant, and the buildings themselves offer a fascinating glimpse of how people lived before the Industrial Revolution.

Don't miss the **Antique Auto and Music Museum**, a colorful jumble of old cars (they have a Tucker), working jukeboxes, player pianos, posters, hand-cranked movie boxes, and other fascinating vintage stuff. Add to all these park attractions a grist mill and a covered bridge and you've got enough to keep you happily busy for several days.

Chattahoochee River/Chattahoochee Nature Center

The 436-mile-long Chattahoochee River flows from the mountains of northern Georgia to the Gulf of Mexico. For fifty miles of its length, it skirts the Atlanta area, and between Lake Lanier to the north and the city limits near Marietta lie a series of parks designed for boating, picnicking, fishing, and hiking.

Summer is raft season on the river. Rent a boat from one of several concessioners (they have some canoes and kayaks, too), buckle up your life preserver, and you're off, floating down the slow-moving waters. Close your eyes and feel the sun on your face; this is a great way to spend an afternoon.

Your options on land are just as pleasant. Fly a kite or throw a frisbee in one of the park meadows; savor a picnic lunch in a leafy glen or go for a hike in riverbank woods. The **Cochran Shoals** park, off I-285 near its intersection with I-75, has a 3-mile fitness trail with 22 exercise stations along the way; other parks offer pre-Civil War ruins and beaches (though, because of its temperature and currents, swimming in the river is not recommended).

The city of **Roswell**, just to the north of the river and 20 miles north of Atlanta, is full of stately antebellum homes, landmarks, and quaint shops. Here, too, is the **Chattahoochee Nature Center**. Nestled in a semirural area on the banks of the river are acres of woodland and marsh, nature trails, and wildlife galore. The Center building houses a truly outstanding store, with books, toys, and all kinds of equipment for the budding naturalist, plus a kids' learning and play corner and a mini-zoo with

turtles, snakes, and even an opposum. Outside, by peaceful Kingfisher Pond, ducks eat out of your hand while curious swans watch and shadowy fish dart here and there under the surface of the water. Not to be missed.

Marietta and Kennesaw

To the northwest of Atlanta (take 1-75). Marietta is by far the bigger of the two communities and boasts a historical downtown (town square, old homes, arty shops, churches) surrounded—as is the case with much of Atlanta and environs—by a seemingly endless suburban sprawl of highways, gas stations, and shopping centers. The **National Cemetery** here, founded in 1866, is the final resting place for more than 10,000 Union soldiers; there's a Confederate cemetery with 3,000 graves nearby. On a less historical note, there's also a 35-acre **White Water** park here where, during summer months, you can body-surf, shoot rapids, slip down a water slide, or bob in an inner tube.

Kennesaw, to the north, is a much smaller town. Set in gently rolling hills, it gives you a sense of what much of this country must have been like before the explosion of development in this century. The **Big Shanty Museum** downtown houses "The General," a Civil War locomotive that was hijacked by Union troops (the subsequent chase was the inspiration for the Disney movie *The Great Locomotive Chase*). The engine and some related Civil War paraphernalia (there's a video, too, about the history of the raid) pretty much constitute the museum, but if you're a railroad buff, it's worth a stop.

Also in Kennesaw: not one but two doll museums. The **Mauldin Doll Museum** has five

rooms crammed with over 4,000 dolls. The Many are very old, but most are twentieth century. There are advertising dolls, cartoon dolls from Popeye to Roger Rabbit, movie dolls (Scarlett O'Hara, Dorothy from *The Wizard of Oz*), as well as just plain doll-dolls of every description. Most fascinating, however, are the character dolls, among them Elvis, Winston Churchill, and Muhammad Ali. Just down the street, in the KOA campground, is the **Doll Gallery,** a collection similar in size and scope.

A few words of warning about the river: be careful not to get too cold—lowering your body temperature can be dangerous. Wear enough clothing, and be prepared for changes in the weather. Know your put-in and take-out points, and let other people know what they are.

On this wooded ridge, Confederate troops under General Joseph Johnson battled Sherman's Union soldiers for several weeks in a last-ditch attempt to save Atlanta. The Northerners lost 3,000 men, the Confederates only 500, but Sherman eventually went around the mountain to the east and closed in on the city.

Kennesaw Mountain National Battlefield

This is the site of one of the most important battles of the 1864 Atlanta campaign of the Civil War. A century and a quarter later, Kennesaw Mountain is quiet, wooded countryside. Still, it's an eerie feeling to stand in a place where so many men died. A few silent cannons dot the meadow in front of the visitors' center; inside, there's a good slide show about the history of the battle. You can hike or drive (there are a lot of good hikes in the park) to the top of the peak, where old guns and earthworks still remain. If the day is clear, you can even make out the hump of Stone Mountain many miles to the southeast.

Six Flags Over Georgia

If you enjoy being scared witless on rides with names like Free Fall and the Great American Scream Machine, this 330-acre amusement park just off I-20 west of the city is the place for you. Here is the triple-loop Mind Bender roller coaster as well as the brand-new Z Force coaster that simulates flight with six speeding, turning vertical dives—just two of more than 100 rides and attractions. Say hello to Bugs Bunny; go dancing; take in a musical revue or a concert at the Southern Star Ampitheatre. Then crawl home, exhausted and content.

Southeastern Railway Museum in Duluth

There's no sign by the road, no office or gift shop, just a field full of 30-plus vintage train cars and engines that you can climb around on (at least, there's no sign saying you can't). Only one or two have been fully restored, and the rest are pretty funky. Steam engine rides are offered on weekends once a month in the summer.

11. Day Trips

here's enough doing in the Atlanta area to keep you busy for weeks. However, if you've got a car and are itching to explore more of Georgia, here are a few suggestions for excursions a bit farther afield.

Lake Lanier
An hour north of the city, this huge lake offers all sorts of outdoor fun. Here you can fish, swim, sail, ski, or just laze in the sun. Lake Lanier Islands at the southern edge of the lake has all the comforts of a big resort: a hotel, camping, horseback riding, golf, restaurants, even a water park and natural history museum!

The Northern Mountains

Here are lush woods, white-water rivers, and the Blue Ridge Mountains rolling hill after valley as far as you can see. The 2,100-mile-long Appalachian trail begins here at Springer Mountain (if you hiked its whole length, you'd end up in Maine). There are Indian mounds at **Etowah**, gold mining at **Dahlonega**, an Alpine village at **Helen**, automobile racing at **Road Atlanta** in Gainesville, and parks galore. If you're really into driving, check out **Chickamauga-Chattanooga National Military Park** on the Tennessee border, with 5,200 acres of Civil War battlefields. And, if you're in Cleveland, stop in at **Babyland General Hospital**, birthplace of the original Cabbage Patch dolls. Here, if you're lucky, you can adopt a one-of-a kind "baby" to take home.

Calloway Gardens

Seventy-five miles to the southwest of Atlanta, this big resort has woodlands, nature trails, golf, a lake, and a wonderful new pavilion full of butterflies.

Atlanta International Raceway

Twenty-five miles south of the city in Hampton. Get your ears blasted by NASCAR races. For funny cars and top fuel dragsters, check out **New Atlanta Dragway** in Commerce, an hour's drive to the northeast.

12. A Look Back

OK, so you're ready to go home. Chances are your head is crammed with great memories and your suitcase stuffed with all sorts of wonderful gifts you bought along the way. Did you create a bolt of lightning at SCITREK? Spy your favorite newscaster at CNN? Get a sunburn on the Chattahoochee or laryngitis from yelling at Six Flags? Whatever you did, it was probably a lot of fun.

When you look back, you'll probably wonder how you crammed so many experiences into your trip. But then, that's the fun of traveling. Your energy goes up; you're ready for just about anything. And, hopefully, you end up just a little bit better person for all the new sights you've seen and experiences you've had.

Atlanta is a city that looks a lot like some other cities at first view—big, brash, and busy. Now that you've visited, you know that that's just the surface. Old and new make exciting patterns here, and because the city's growing, there are always new attractions to look forward to. So as your plane arches into the sky or your car zips along the freeway, look out the window and say good-bye.

Chances are, you'll be back!

13. Calendar

In addition to its year-round attractions, Atlanta offers many special events and festivals of interest to visitors. The following is a selective list of annual goings-on you might be interested in, if you're in town. For additional, up-to-the-minute information, consult the local papers or call the Atlanta Convention and Visitors Bureau at (404) 521-6600.

January
Martin Luther King, Jr., Festival and March
Atlanta Hawks basketball

February
Atlanta Jugglers Association Festival, Grady High School, midtown

March
St. Patrick's Day Parade, downtown
St. Patrick's Day Shindig, Stone Mountain Village

April
Dogwood Festival: balloon races, concerts, games
Atlanta Historical Society Spring Festival, Buckhead: clowns, magicians, flowers, games

Martin Luther King, Jr., Memorial Weekend: ceremonies marking the anniversary of King's assassination
Sweet Auburn Good Times Festival
Inman Park Festival and tour of homes
Druid Hills Home and Garden Tour
Baseball season begins for the Atlanta Braves
Midtown tour of homes
Virginia-Highland tour of homes
Ansley Park tour of homes
Old South Celebration, Stone Mountain Park

May
West End Festival, West End
Kool Jazz Festival, Piedmont Park
Springfest, Stone Mountain Park
Armed Forces Festival, Lockheed/Dobbins Air Force Base, Marietta

All Summer Long

Laser show nightly at dusk, Stone Mountain Park

Atlanta Symphony Orchestra concerts, Sundays, Piedmont Park

Georgia Shakespeare Festival, Oglethorpe University

Concerts in Decatur Square, Decatur (these occur in the spring and fall as well)

Summer festival, Center for Puppetry Arts, midtown

June

Festival of the Arts, Stone Mountain Village

Art Show, Jonesboro

July

10K Peachtree Road Race, July 4, from Lenox Square to Piedmont Park

Salute 2 America July 4th Parade, the biggest in the country

July 4th fireworks, Decatur Square, Decatur

September

Art in the Park, Labor Day, Marietta

Avondale Estates Fun Run, Labor Day

Football season starts, Georgia Tech and Atlanta Falcons

Oakland Cemetery Anniversary Celebration

Grant Park tour of homes

Roswell Arts and Crafts Festival, Roswell

Yellow Daisy Festival, Stone Mountain Park

October

Arts Festival of Atlanta, Piedmont Park

Morningside tour of homes

Fall Festival, Fernbank Science Center, Decatur

Cotton Days, Marietta

Youth Days and Festival, Roswell

Scottish Highland Games, Stone Mountain Park

Fall Festival and annual reenactment of the Battle of Jonesboro, Jonesboro

November

Virginia-Highlands Artists and Craftsmen Fair

Scottish Rite Festival, Georgia Tech: concert, footrace, and traditional Georgia Tech-Georgia Junior Varsity football game

Lighting of Rich's department store Christmas tree downtown, Thanksgiving night

December

Christmas cheer and special events galore, including:

Macy's Christmas Parade and Festival of Trees

Peach Bowl Parade

West End Christmas Festival and Christmas Open House at the Wren's Nest

Christmas Candlelight Tour, Grant Park

Marietta Christmas home tour

Lighting of state Christmas tree at the Governor's mansion, Buckhead

Candlelight tour of Tullie Smith House, Atlanta Historical Society, Buckhead

Festival of Nine Lessons and Carols: traditional Christmas music program at Emory University

Candlelight tour of homes, Decatur

Christmas Festival and home tour, Roswell

Sugar Plum Festival, Stone Mountain Village

Christmas at the Antebellum Plantation, Stone Mountain Park

Appendix

Atlanta Botanical Garden
Piedmont Avenue at the Prado, N.E.
(404)876-5858
Hours: 9:00 a.m.–6:00 p.m. Tues.–Sat.;
  noon–6:00 p.m. Sun. Closed Mon.
Admission: Adults $2.00; senior citizens and
  children 6–12 $1.00. Children under 12 and
  members free. No admission charge Thurs.
  1:30 p.m.–6:00 p.m.

Atlanta Cyclorama
800 Cherokee Avenue, S.E.
(404)624-1071
Hours: 9:30 a.m.–5:30 p.m. May–Sept.;
  9:30 a.m.–4:30 p.m. Oct.–Apr. Closed Martin
  Luther King Day, Thanksgiving, Christmas,
  and New Year's Day.
Admission: Adults $3.50; senior citizens $3.00;
  children 6-12 $2.00.

Atlanta Historical Society
3101 Andrews Drive, N.W.
(404)261-1837
Hours: 9:00 a.m.–5:30 p.m. Mon.–Sat.;
  noon–5:00 p.m. Sun. Tours of Tully Smith
  House and Swan House every half-hour.
Admission: Adults $4.50; students and senior cit-
  izens $4.00; children 6–12 $2.00.
Note: There is also a small branch of the Atlanta
  Historical Society downtown, at 140 Peachtree
  Street, N.E., (404)238-0655. Hours are
  10:00 a.m.–6:00 p.m. Mon.–Sat., and admission is free.

Atlanta International Raceway
Hampton, GA 30228
(404)946-4211

Atlanta Marriott Marquis
265 Peachtree Center Avenue, N.E.
(404)521-0000

Atlanta Preservation Center
401 The Flatiron Building
84 Peachtree Street, N.W.
(404)522-4345
Offers guided walking tours of six historic areas
  of Atlanta, April–October. Neighborhoods
  included are State Capitol and Underground
  Atlanta; Fairlie-Poplar District; Fox Theatre
  District; Inman Park; Oakland Cemetery; and
  Wren's Nest/West End. Call for assembly points
  and schedule. Each tour requires a $3.00 dona-
  tion per person.

Afro-American Panoramic Experience (APEX)
135 Auburn Avenue, N.E.
(404)521-APEX
Hours: 10:00 a.m.–5:00 p.m. Tues.–Sat.;
  10:00 a.m.–6:00 p.m. Wed.; 1:00 p.m.–5:00 p.m.
  Sun. Closed Mon.
Admission: Adults $2.00; students and senior cit-
  izens $1.00; children under 5 and members
  free.

Babyland General Hospital
19 Underwood Street
Cleveland, GA 30528
(404)865-2171
Hours: 8:30 a.m.–5:00 p.m. Mon.–Sat.;
  1:00 p.m.–5:00 p.m. Sun. Admission free.

Big Shanty Museum
2829 Cherokee Street
Kennesaw, GA 30144
(404)427-2117

Hours: 9:30 a.m.—5:30 p.m. Mon.–Sat.;
noon–5:30 p.m. Sun. and daily Dec.–Feb.
Closed Easter, Thanksgiving, Christmas and
New Year's Day.
Admission: Adults $2.50; children 7–15 $1.00.

Callanwolde Fine Arts Center

980 Briarcliff Road, N.E.
(404)872-5338
Hours: 10:00 a.m.–5:00 p.m. Mon.–Sat. Call for
schedule of arts events.
Admission: No charge for entry to gallery or gift
shop. Tours of the mansion and grounds, by
reservation, are adults $1.50, children $.50.

Calloway Gardens

Pine Mountain, GA 31822
(404)663-2281; 1-800-282-8181
Hours: Gardens open 7:00 a.m.–7:00 p.m. daily in
summer; 9:00 a.m.–5:00 p.m. in winter. Beach
open 9:00 a.m.–9:00 p.m. Memorial Day–Labor
Day.
Admission: Adults $4.00; children 6–11 $1.00.
Additional charge for beach and sports
facilities.

Carter Presidential Center

1 Copenhill, N.E.
(404)331-0296
Hours: Library and museum open 9:00 a.m.–
4:45 p.m. Mon.–Sat.; noon–4:45 p.m. Sun.
Closed Thanksgiving, Christmas, and New
Year's Day.
Admission: Adults $2.50; senior citizens $1.50;
children under 16 free.

Center for Puppetry Arts

1404 Spring Street, N.W.
(404)873-3089 business office; 873-3391 box
office
Hours: 9:00 a.m.–noon Mon.–Fri.; 10:00 a.m.–
3:30 p.m. Sat. Call for performance schedule.
Admission: $1.00 donation requested. Separate
admission for performances.

Chattahoochee River National Recreation Area

Superintendent, 1900 Northridge Road
Dunwoody, GA 30338
(404)394-8335, 952-4419 park information
(404)394-7912 additional information

Chattahoochee Nature Center

9135 Willeo Road
Roswell, GA 30075
(404)992-2055

Hours: 9:00 a.m.–5:00 p.m. Mon.–Sat.;
10:00 a.m.–5:00 p.m. Sun.
Admission: Adults $1.00; senior citizens and chil-
dren ages 5-15 $.50; members free.

CNN Center

1 CNN Center
Marietta Street at Techwood Drive, N.W.
(404)827-1825; 827-2300 tour information
Hours: 45-minute tours are given on the hour,
10:00 a.m.–5:00 p.m. Mon.–Fri.; 10:00 a.m.–
4:00 p.m. weekends.
Admission: Adults $4.00; senior citizens and stu-
dents under 18 $2.00.

Doll Gallery

at KOA Atlanta North
2000 Old U.S. Highway 41
Kennesaw, GA 30144
(404)427-2406
Call for hours and admission fees.

Ebenezer Baptist Church

407 Auburn Avenue, N.E.
(404)688-7263
Hours: 9:30 a.m.–noon, 1:30 p.m.–4:30 p.m.
Mon.–Fri. Call for Saturday hours. Sunday wor-
ship services open to the public. Donations
accepted.

Emory Museum of Art and Archaeology

Michael C. Carlos Hall
Emory University Quadrangle
(404)727-7522
Hours: 10:00 a.m.–4:30 p.m. Tues.–Sat.; noon–
5:00 p.m. Sun. Admission free, but donations
welcome.

Fernbank Science Center

156 Heaton Park Drive, N.E.
(404)378-4311
Hours: *Forest* open 2:00 p.m.–5:00 p.m. Mon.–
Fri.; 10:00 a.m.–5:00 p.m. Sat.; 2:00 p.m.–
5:00 p.m. Sun. *Exhibit hall* open 8:30
a.m.–5:00 p.m. Mon.; 8:30 a.m.–10:00 p.m.
Tues.–Fri.; 10:00 a.m.–5:00 p.m. Sat.; 1:00
p.m.–5:00 p.m. Sun. *Planetarium* programs
begin at 8:00 p.m. Tues.–Fri.; 11:00 a.m. and
3:00 p.m. Sat.; 3:00 p.m. Sun. There are also
shows at 3:00 p.m. Wed. and Fri. except during
summer. *Observatory* is open Thurs. and Fri.
evenings only. Schedule depends on weather;
call for hours.
Admission: Planetarium shows: Adults $2.00;
students $1.00. All other facilities free.

Fernbank Museum of Natural History
To open in 1991
For information call (404)378-0127

Fox Theatre
660 Peachtree Street, N.E.
(404)881-1977 box office
Tours available through Atlanta Preservation
Center. Call (404)522-4345 for details.

Georgia Governor's Mansion
391 West Paces Ferry Road, N.E.
(404)261-1776
Hours: 10:00 a.m.–11:30 a.m. Tues.–Thurs.
Admission free.

Herndon Home
587 University Place, N.W.
(404)581-9813
Hours: Tours given 10:00 a.m.–4:00 p.m. Tues.–
Sat. Admission free.

High Museum of Art
1280 Peachtree Street, N.E.
(404)892-3600; 892-HIGH
Hours: 10:00 a.m.–5:00 p.m. Tues.–Sat.; 10:00
a.m.–9:00 p.m. Wed.; noon–5:00 p.m. Sun.
Admission: Adults $4.00; senior citizens and stu-
dents with I.D.'s $2.00; children 6–17 $1.00. No
charge on Thursdays.

High Museum of Art at Georgia-Pacific Center
133 Peachtree Street, N.E.
(404)577-6940
Hours: 11:00 a.m.–5:00 p.m. Mon.–Fri. Admission free.

Hyatt Regency Atlanta
265 Peachtree Street, N.E.
(404)577-1234

Kennesaw Mountain National Battlefield Park
Old Highway 41 and Stilesboro Road
Marietta, GA 30061
(404)427-4686
Hours: 8:30 a.m.–5:00 p.m. daily. Front gates
close at 8:00 p.m. Apr.–Oct.; 6:00 p.m. Oct.–
Apr. Admission free.

Lake Lanier Islands
P.O. Box 605
Buford, GA 30518
(404)945-6701
Hours: Open all day every day.
Admission: $3.00 per car; $15.00 annual pass.
Water park: $7.50 per person; children under 5
free. Annual pass $30.00 per person.

Lenox Square
3393 Peachtree Road, N.E.
(404)233-6767
Hours: 10:00 a.m.–9:30 p.m. Mon.–Sat.;
12:30 p.m.–6:00 p.m. Sun.

MARTA
(404)848-4711 (schedule and route information)
Hours: Trains operate from approximately 5:30 a.m.
to 12:30 a.m. daily.

Martin Luther King, Jr., Birth Home
501 Auburn Avenue, N.E.
(404)331-3919
Hours: 10:00 a.m.–4:30 p.m. daily June–Labor
Day; 10:00 a.m.–3:30 p.m. daily Labor Day–
May. Admission free.

**Martin Luther King, Jr., Center for Nonviolent
Social Change, Inc.**
449 Auburn Avenue, N.E.
(404)524-1956
Hours: 9:00 a.m.–5:30 p.m. Mon.–Fri.; 10:00 a.m.–
5:30 p.m. weekends (Oct.–May). 9:00 a.m.–
8:00 p.m. Mon.–Fri.; 10:00 a.m.–8:00 p.m.
weekends (June–Aug.) Admission free. $1.00
fee for viewing film on Dr. King.

Mauldin Doll Museum
2238 Whitfield Place
Kennesaw, GA 30144
(404)426-8818; 428-4931
Hours: 10:00 a.m.–4:00 p.m. Tues.–Sat.

New Atlanta Dragway
Commerce, GA
(404)335-2301

New Georgia Railroad
Georgia Building Authority
1 Martin Luther King, Jr. Drive, S.W.
(404)656-0769
Call for schedules and reservations.

Oakland Cemetery
248 Oakland Avenue, S.E.
(404)577-8163
Hours: Open daily sunrise to sunset. Admission free.

Peachtree Center
Bounded by Baker, Ellis, Williams and Courtland
Streets, N.E.
(404)659-0800

Phipps Plaza
3500 Peachtree at Lenox Road, N.E.
(404)261-7910

Piedmont Park
Park Drive, N.E.
(404)872-1507

Road Atlanta
Georgia Highway 53
Gainesville, GA 30517
(404)881-8233

SCITREK·Science and Technology Museum of Atlanta
395 Piedmont Avenue, N.E.
(404)522-5500
Hours: 10:00 a.m.–5:00 p.m. Tues.–Sun. Closed Easter, Thanksgiving, and Christmas.
Admission: Families $15.00; adults over 18 $5.00; children 3–17 $3.00; children under 3 free.

Six Flags Over Georgia
7561 Six Flags Road, S.W., at I-20 West
Mableton, GA 30059
(404)739-3400
Hours: Open daily Memorial Day–late Aug.; weekends only mid–March through Memorial Day and late Aug.–Oct. Daily hours vary.
Admission: Adult one-day ticket $17.50; 2-day ticket $19.95. Seniors 55 and older and children 42″ and under $10.95. Children under 2 free.

Southeastern Railway Museum
3966 Buford Highway
Duluth, GA 30136-4135
(404)476-2013
Hours: 9:00 a.m.–5:00 p.m. Sat. Steam train operates the third weekend of each month, May–Oct. Admission free.

State Capitol
Capitol Hill at Washington Street, S.E.
(404)656-2844
Hours: 8:00 a.m.–5:30 p.m. Mon.–Fri.; 10:00 a.m.–2:00 p.m. Sat.; 1:00 p.m.–3:00 p.m. Sun. Weekday tours on the hour, 10:00 a.m.–4:00 p.m. (except noon). Admission free.

Stone Mountain Park
P.O. Box 778
Stone Mountain, GA 30086
(404)498-5600
Hours: Park open 6:00 a.m.–midnight daily. Attractions open 10:00 a.m.–8:00 p.m. June–Aug.; 10:00 a.m.–5:30 p.m. Sept.–May.
Admission: Car $5.00, $20.00 annual permit. Each major attraction: Adults $2.50, children (3–11) $1.50.

Underground Atlanta
Peachtree Street at Alabama Street
Consult directory for information number.

Varsity Diner
61 North Avenue, N.W., across from Georgia Tech
(404)881-1706
Hours: 7:00 a.m.–12:30 a.m. Sun.–Thurs.; 7:00 a.m.–2:00 a.m. Fri.–Sat.

Westin Peachtree Plaza
Peachtree Street and International Boulevard, N.W.
(404)659-1400

Whitewater Park
North Marietta Parkway
Marietta, GA 30062
(404)424-WAVE
Hours: Park opens first weekend in May. Open weekends in May and Sept.; daily 10:00 a.m.–10:00 p.m. Memorial Day-Labor Day.
Admission: One-, two-, and three-day admissions: Adults $12.99 to $20.80; children $7.99 to $14.55.

Woodruff Arts Center
1280 Peachtree Street, N.E.
(404)892-3600; 892-2414 box office
Call for schedule of performances.

Wren's Nest
1050 Gordon Street, S.W.
(404)753-8535/6
Hours: 10:00 a.m.–5:00 p.m. Tues.–Sat.; 2:00 p.m.–5:00 p.m. Sun. (last tour at 4:00 p.m.).
Admission: Adults $3.00; senior citizens and teenagers $2.00; children (4–12) $1.00.

ZOO Atlanta
800 Cherokee Avenue, S.E.
(404)624-5678
Hours: 10:00 a.m.–5:00 p.m. daily. Ticket office closes at 4:00 p.m. 10:00 a.m.–6:00 p.m. weekends, Memorial Day–Labor Day. Closed New Year's Day, Martin Luther King Day, Thanksgiving, and Christmas.
Admission: Adults $5.75; children (3–11) $3.00. Under age 3 free.

Albuquerque Academy
MIDDLE SCHOOL LIBRARY
6400 Wyoming Blvd. N.E.
Albuquerque, NM 87109

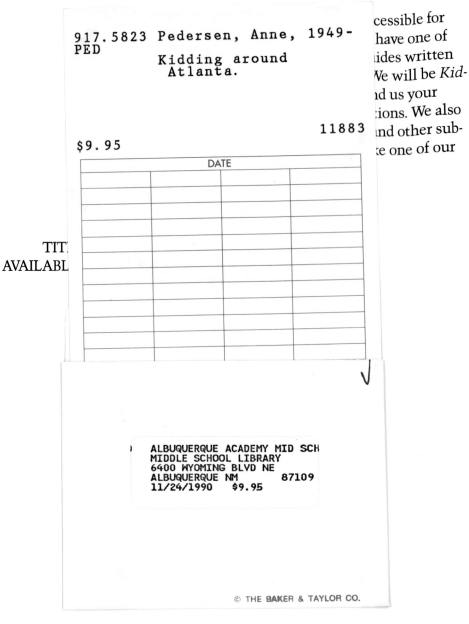

917.5823 Pedersen, Anne, 1949-
PED

    Kidding around
      Atlanta.

11883

$9.95

cessible for
have one of
uides written
We will be *Kid-*
nd us your
tions. We also
nd other sub-
e one of our

DATE

TIT
AVAILABL

   ALBUQUERQUE ACADEMY MID SCH
   MIDDLE SCHOOL LIBRARY
   6400 WYOMING BLVD NE
   ALBUQUERQUE NM   87109
   11/24/1990 $9.95

© THE BAKER & TAYLOR CO.